THE S
OF

God

with us

AN ADVENT DEVOTIONAL

As you experience the Advent season,
The Story of God with Us
will help you prepare your heart to receive and
celebrate all that God unveils in his Story.

You will travel through the words of the Bible,
discovering God's redemptive plan and the depth
of his love for you through the gift he sent at
Christmas. May you and your family have a special
journey together celebrating God's gift to you,
his one and only Son.

ZONDERVAN®

ZONDERVAN

The Story of God With Us
Copyright © 2013 Zondervan

Requests for information should be addressed to:

Zondervan, *Grand Rapids, Michigan 49530*

ISBN 978-0-310-62047-1

Content excerpted from *The Story, NIV*, Copyright © 2011, Zondervan. Used by permission.

Printed in the United States of America

13 14 15 16 17 18 • 17 16 15 14 13 12 11 10 9 8 7 6 5 4 3 2 1

How to Use This Book

Throughout this book, you will see some icons
to help you identify where each verse fits
into bigger picture of *The Story:*

Picture	Portion of *The Story*	Portion of the Bible
✡	*The Story* of Israel	Genesis 12-Malachi
✝	*The Story* of Jesus	Matthew-John

Two sets of scripture references
are provided for each day. The first set of references
are for that day's reading. The second set of references
are additional scriptures for further study.

1ST Sunday IN ADVENT

LORD, prepare my heart to receive you in a special way this Christmas season. The world seems to be so hurried and blind to the reality of YOU.

May my heart and mind stay focused on you and the gift of Salvation that you bring into the world. I pray that you lead me to take refuge in you and that I will rest in the comfort you bring. Keep my heart in prayer for those that you put in my path. May each of us experience the miracle of Christmas and receive the gift of YOU with us.

God with Us

A shoot will come up from the stump of Jesse; from his roots a Branch will bear fruit. The Spirit of the Lord will rest on him—the Spirit of wisdom and of understanding, the Spirit of counsel and of might, the Spirit of the knowledge and fear of the Lord—and he will delight in the fear of the Lord.

He will not judge by what he sees with his eyes, or decide by what he hears with his ears; but with righteousness he will judge the needy, with justice he will give decisions for the poor of the earth. He will strike the earth with the rod of his mouth; with the breath of his lips he will slay the wicked. Righteousness will be his belt and faithfulness the sash around his waist.

Therefore the Lord himself will give you a sign: The virgin will conceive and give birth to a son, and will call him Immanuel (God with Us.)

✡ ISAIAH 11:1-5, ISAIAH 7:14
✝ LUKE 3:32, MATTHEW 1:18-23

Take Refuge in Him

I will proclaim the Lord's decree: He said to me, "You are my son; today I have become your father. Ask me, and I will make the nations your inheritance, the ends of the earth your possession. You will break them with a rod of iron; you will dash them to pieces like pottery."

Therefore, you kings, be wise; be warned, you rulers of the earth. Serve the Lord with fear and celebrate his rule with trembling. Kiss his son, or he will be angry and your way will lead to your destruction, for his wrath can flare up in a moment. Blessed are all who take refuge in him.

✡ PSALM 2:7-12
✝ MATTHEW 3:17

A Covenant for the People

"Here is my servant, whom I uphold, my chosen one in whom I delight; I will put my Spirit on him, and he will bring justice to the nations. He will not shout or cry out, or raise his voice in the streets. A bruised reed he will not break, and a smoldering wick he will not snuff out. In faithfulness he will bring forth justice; he will not falter or be discouraged till he establishes justice on earth. In his teaching the islands will put their hope."

This is what God the Lord says—the Creator of the heavens, who stretches them out, who spreads out the earth with all that springs from it, who gives breath to its people, and life to those who walk on it: "I, the Lord, have called you in righteousness; I will take hold of your hand. I will keep you and will make you to be a covenant for the people and a light for the Gentiles, to open eyes that are blind, to free captives from prison and to release from the dungeon those who sit in darkness."

✡ ISAIAH 42:1-7
✝ MATTHEW 12:18-21, LUKE 2:32

The Holy One of Israel, Your Savior

But now, this is what the LORD says—he who created you, Jacob, he who formed you, Israel: "Do not fear, for I have redeemed you; I have summoned you by name; you are mine. When you pass through the waters, I will be with you; and when you pass through the rivers, they will not sweep over you. When you walk through the fire, you will not be burned; the flames will not set you ablaze. For I am the Lord your God, the Holy One of Israel, your Savior; I give Egypt for your ransom, Cush and Seba in your stead. Since you are precious and honored in my sight, and because I love you, I will give people in exchange for you, nations in exchange for your life. Do not be afraid, for I am with you; I will bring your children from the east and gather you from the west. I will say to the north, 'Give them up!' and to the south, 'Do not hold them back.' Bring my sons from afar and my daughters from the ends of the earth—everyone who is called by my name, whom I created for my glory, whom I formed and made."

Lead out those who have eyes but are blind, who have ears but are deaf. All the nations gather together and the peoples assemble. Which of their gods foretold this and proclaimed to us the former things? Let them bring in their witnesses to prove they were right, so that others may hear and say, "It is true." "You are my witnesses," declares the Lord, "and my servant whom I have chosen, so that you may know and believe me and understand that I am he. Before me no god was formed, nor will there be one after me. I, even I, am the Lord, and apart from me there is no savior. I have revealed and saved and proclaimed—I, and not some foreign god among you. You are my witnesses," declares the Lord, "that I am God. Yes, and from ancient days I am he. No one can deliver out of my hand. When I act, who can reverse it?"

✡ ISAIAH 43:1-13

✝ ACTS 4:12

A Light for the Gentiles

Listen to me, you islands; hear this, you distant nations: Before I was born the Lord called me; from my mother's womb he has spoken my name. He made my mouth like a sharpened sword, in the shadow of his hand he hid me; he made me into a polished arrow and concealed me in his quiver. He said to me, "You are my servant, Israel, in whom I will display my splendor." But I said, "I have labored in vain; I have spent my strength for nothing at all. Yet what is due me is in the Lord's hand, and my reward is with my God."

And now the Lord says—he who formed me in the womb to be his servant to bring Jacob back to him and gather Israel to himself, for I am honored in the eyes of the Lord and my God has been my strength—he says: "It is too small a thing for you to be my servant to restore the tribes of Jacob and bring back those of Israel I have kept. I will also make you a light for the Gentiles that my salvation may reach to the ends of the earth."

This is what the Lord says—the Redeemer and Holy One of Israel—to him who was despised and abhorred by the nation, to the servant of rulers: "Kings will see you and stand up, princes will see and bow down, because of the Lord, who is faithful, the Holy One of Israel, who has chosen you."

— ✺ —

✡ ISAIAH 49:1-7

✟ LUKE 2:29-32, ACTS 13:47

Wonderful Counselor, Mighty God, Everlasting Father, Prince of Peace

The people walking in darkness have seen a great light; on those living in the land of deep darkness a light has dawned. You have enlarged the nation and increased their joy; they rejoice before you as people rejoice at the harvest, as warriors rejoice when dividing the plunder. For as in the day of Midian's defeat, you have shattered the yoke that burdens them, the bar across their shoulders, the rod of their oppressor. Every warrior's boot used in battle and every garment rolled in blood will be destined for burning, will be fuel for the fire. For to us a child is born, to us a son is given, and the government will be on his shoulders. And he will be called Wonderful Counselor, Mighty God, Everlasting Father, Prince of Peace. Of the greatness of his government and peace there will be no end. He will reign on David's throne and over his kingdom, establishing and upholding it with justice and righteousness from that time on and forever. The zeal of the Lord Almighty will accomplish this.

✡ ISAIAH 9:2-7
✝ LUKE 1:32-33

The Lord Has Comforted His People

How beautiful on the mountains are the feet of those who bring good news, who proclaim peace, who bring good tidings, who proclaim salvation, who say to Zion, "Your God reigns!" Listen! Your watchmen lift up their voices; together they shout for joy. When the Lord returns to Zion, they will see it with their own eyes. Burst into songs of joy together, you ruins of Jerusalem, for the Lord has comforted his people, he has redeemed Jerusalem. The Lord will lay bare his holy arm in the sight of all the nations, and all the ends of the earth will see the salvation of our God.

Depart, depart, go out from there! Touch no unclean thing! Come out from it and be pure, you who carry the articles of the Lord's house. But you will not leave in haste or go in flight; for the Lord will go before you, the God of Israel will be your rear guard.

See, my servant will act wisely; he will be raised and lifted up and highly exalted. Just as there were many who were appalled at him—his appearance was so disfigured beyond that of any human being and his form marred beyond human likeness—so he will sprinkle many nations, and kings will shut their mouths because of him. For what they were not told, they will see, and what they have not heard, they will understand.

———————————— ✿ ————————————

✡ ISAIAH 52:7-15

✝ LUKE 4:14-15, REVELATION 1:5

2ND *Sunday* IN ADVENT

Father, the day is drawing closer for celebrating your birth. I am completely overwhelmed by the enormous love you have for me. I stand in awe of you and the way you revealed your plan long ago through the prophets.

May I daily meditate on your words and the revelation of your everlasting covenant.

Help me comprehend the reality of the sacrifice you made on my behalf. Draw me to spend time this week in your presence thanking you for taking my iniquities upon yourself. I am justified only because of what you have done for me.

Prepare my heart to rejoice in you and spread your love all the days of my life.

My Righteous Servant Will Justify Many

Who has believed our message and to whom has the arm of the Lord been revealed? He grew up before him like a tender shoot, and like a root out of dry ground. He had no beauty or majesty to attract us to him, nothing in his appearance that we should desire him. He was despised and rejected by mankind, a man of suffering, and familiar with pain. Like one from whom people hide their faces he was despised, and we held him in low esteem.

Surely he took up our pain and bore our suffering, yet we considered him punished by God, stricken by him, and afflicted. But he was pierced for our transgressions, he was crushed for our iniquities; the punishment that brought us peace was on him, and by his wounds we are healed. We all, like sheep, have gone astray, each of us has turned to our own way; and the Lord has laid on him the iniquity of us all.

He was oppressed and afflicted, yet he did not open his mouth; he was led like a lamb to the slaughter, and as a sheep before its shearers is silent, so he did not open his mouth. By oppression and judgment he was taken away. Yet who of his generation protested? For he was cut off from the land of the living; for the transgression of my people he was punished. He was assigned a grave with the wicked and with the rich in his death, though he had done no violence, nor was any deceit in his mouth.

Yet it was the Lord's will to crush him and cause him to suffer, and though the Lord makes his life an offering for sin, he will see his offspring and prolong his days, and the will of the Lord will prosper in his hand. After he has suffered, he will see the light of life and be satisfied; by his knowledge my righteous servant will justify many, and he will bear their iniquities. Therefore I will give him a portion among the great, and he will divide the spoils with the strong, because he poured out his life unto death, and was numbered with the transgressors. For he bore the sin of many, and made intercession for the transgressors.

✡ ISAIAH 53:1-12

✝ 1 PETER 2:24, LUKE 23:33,
GALATIANS 1:4

The Son Is the Radiance of God's Glory

In the past God spoke to our ancestors through the prophets at many times and in various ways, but in these last days he has spoken to us by his Son, whom he appointed heir of all things, and through whom also he made the universe. The Son is the radiance of God's glory and the exact representation of his being, sustaining all things by his powerful word. After he had provided purification for sins, he sat down at the right hand of the Majesty in heaven. So he became as much superior to the angels as the name he has inherited is superior to theirs.

For to which of the angels did God ever say,

"You are my Son; today I have become your Father"?

Or again,

"I will be his Father, and he will be my Son"?

And again, when God brings his firstborn into the world, he says,

"Let all God's angels worship him."
In speaking of the angels he says,
"He makes his angels spirits, and his servants
flames of fire."

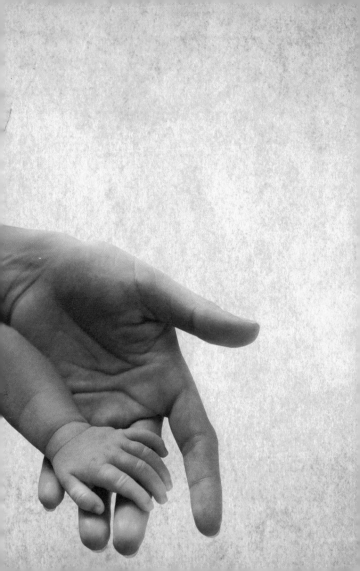

But about the Son he says,

"Your throne, O God, will last for ever and ever; a scepter of justice will be the scepter of your kingdom. You have loved righteousness and hated wickedness; therefore God, your God, has set you above your companions by anointing you with the oil of joy."

He also says,

"In the beginning, Lord, you laid the foundations of the earth, and the heavens are the work of your hands. They will perish, but you remain; they will all wear out like a garment. You will roll them up like a robe; like a garment they will be changed. But you remain the same, and your years will never end."

✝ HEBREWS 1:1-12

✡ PSALM 2:7, PSALM 110:1

An Everlasting Covenant

The Spirit of the Sovereign LORD is on me, because the LORD has anointed me to proclaim good news to the poor. He has sent me to bind up the brokenhearted, to proclaim freedom for the captives and release from darkness for the prisoners, to proclaim the year of the LORD's favor and the day of vengeance of our God, to comfort all who mourn, and provide for those who grieve in Zion—to bestow on them a crown of beauty instead of ashes, the oil of joy instead of mourning, and a garment of praise instead of a spirit of despair. They will be called oaks of righteousness, a planting of the LORD for the display of his splendor. They will rebuild the ancient ruins and restore the places long devastated; they will renew the ruined cities that have been devastated for generations.

Strangers will shepherd your flocks; foreigners will work your fields and vineyards. And you will be called priests of the LORD, you will be named ministers of our God. You will feed on the wealth of nations, and in their riches you will boast. Instead of your shame you will receive a double portion, and instead of disgrace you will rejoice in your inheritance. And so you will inherit a double portion in your land, and everlasting joy will be yours.

"For I, the LORD, love justice; I hate robbery and wrongdoing. In my faithfulness I will reward my people and make an everlasting covenant with them. Their descendants will be known among the nations and their offspring among the peoples. All who see them will acknowledge that they are a people the LORD has blessed." I delight greatly in the LORD; my soul rejoices in my God. For he has clothed me with garments of salvation and arrayed me in a robe of his righteousness, as a bridegroom adorns his head like a priest, and as a bride adorns herself with her jewels. For as the soil makes the sprout come up and a garden causes seeds to grow, so the Sovereign LORD will make righteousness and praise spring up before all nations.

✡ ISAIAH 61:1-11

✝ MATTHEW 3:16-17, JOHN 8:31-32

Out of Bethlehem

But you, Bethlehem Ephrathah, though you are small among the clans of Judah, out of you will come for me one who will be ruler over Israel, whose origins are from of old, from ancient times.

✡ MICAH 5:2

✝ MATTHEW 2:1-2

The Light of All Mankind

In the beginning was the Word, and the Word was with God, and the Word was God. He was with God in the beginning. Through him all things were made; without him nothing was made that has been made. In him was life, and that life was the light of all mankind. The light shines in the darkness, and the darkness has not overcome it.

There was a man sent from God whose name was John. He came as a witness to testify concerning that light, so that through him all might believe. He himself was not the light; he came only as a witness to the light. The true light that gives light to everyone was coming into the world.

He was in the world, and though the world was made through him, the world did not recognize him. He came to that which was his own, but his own did not receive him. Yet to all who did receive him, to those who believed in his name, he gave the right to become children of God— children born not of natural descent, nor of human decision or a husband's will, but born of God.

The Word became flesh and made his dwelling among us. We have seen his glory, the glory of the one and only Son, who came from the Father, full of grace and truth.

✝ JOHN 1:1-14

✡ ISAIAH 9:2

Grace and Truth

For the law was given through Moses; grace and truth
came through Jesus Christ. No one has ever seen God, but
the one and only Son, who is himself God and is in closest
relationship with the Father, has made him known.

✝ JOHN 1:17-18

✡ PSALM 2:7

Prepare for the Lord

In the time of Herod king of Judea there was a priest named Zechariah, who belonged to the priestly division of Abijah; his wife Elizabeth was also a descendant of Aaron. Both of them were righteous in the sight of God, observing all the Lord's commands and decrees blamelessly. But they were childless because Elizabeth was not able to conceive, and they were both very old.

Once when Zechariah's division was on duty and he was serving as priest before God, he was chosen by lot, according to the custom of the priesthood, to go into the temple of the Lord and burn incense. And when the time for the burning of incense came, all the assembled worshipers were praying outside. Then an angel of the Lord appeared to him, standing at the right side of the altar of incense. When Zechariah saw him, he was startled and was gripped with fear. But the angel said to him: "Do not be afraid, Zechariah; your prayer has been heard. Your wife Elizabeth will bear you a son, and you are to call him John. He will be a joy and delight to you, and many will rejoice because of his birth, for he will be great in the sight of the Lord. He is never to take wine or other fermented drink, and he will be filled with the Holy Spirit even before he is born. He will bring back many of the people of Israel to the Lord their God. And he will go on before the Lord, in the spirit and power of Elijah, to turn the hearts of the parents to their children and the disobedient to the wisdom of the righteous—to make ready a people prepared for the Lord."

✝ LUKE 1:5-17

✡ MALACHI 3:1

3RD *Sunday* IN ADVENT

Lord, I come this week asking that you still my heart and my mind and bring me into rest, focusing on the knowledge that YOU alone are God.

Even in the midst of a chaotic world you are the LORD, Almighty, the KING of kings and the LORD of lords, Wonderful Counselor, Mighty God, Everlasting Father, Prince of Peace.

May I deeply understand and share the message of joy to the world, the LORD has come.

May my heart prepare room for you, dear Jesus, Messiah—my Savior, to receive with gratitude the Christmas gift that you give me.

The Lord Has Shown His Favor

Zechariah asked the angel, "How can I be sure of this? I am an old man and my wife is well along in years." The angel said to him, "I am Gabriel. I stand in the presence of God, and I have been sent to speak to you and to tell you this good news. And now you will be silent and not able to speak until the day this happens, because you did not believe my words, which will come true at their appointed time."

Meanwhile, the people were waiting for Zechariah and wondering why he stayed so long in the temple. When he came out, he could not speak to them. They realized he had seen a vision in the temple, for he kept making signs to them but remained unable to speak. When his time of service was completed, he returned home.

After this his wife Elizabeth became pregnant and for five months remained in seclusion. "The Lord has done this for me," she said. "In these days he has shown his favor and taken away my disgrace among the people."

✝ LUKE 1:18-25
✡ DANIEL 8:16

Son of the Most High

In the sixth month of Elizabeth's pregnancy, God sent the angel Gabriel to Nazareth, a town in Galilee, to a virgin pledged to be married to a man named Joseph, a descendant of David. The virgin's name was Mary. The angel went to her and said, "Greetings, you who are highly favored! The Lord is with you." Mary was greatly troubled at his words and wondered what kind of greeting this might be. But the angel said to her, "Do not be afraid, Mary; you have found favor with God. You will conceive and give birth to a son, and you are to call him Jesus. He will be great and will be called the Son of the Most High. The Lord God will give him the throne of his father David, and he will reign over Jacob's descendants forever; his kingdom will never end."

"How will this be," Mary asked the angel, "since I am a virgin?"

The angel answered, "The Holy Spirit will come on you, and the power of the Most High will overshadow you. So the holy one to be born will be called the Son of God. Even Elizabeth your relative is going to have a child in her old age, and she who was said to be unable to conceive is in her sixth month. For no word from God will ever fail."

"I am the Lord's servant," Mary answered. "May your word to me be fulfilled." Then the angel left her.

✝ LUKE 1:26-38

✡ ISAIAH 9:6-7

Conceived from the Holy Spirit

Because Joseph her husband was faithful to the law, and yet did not want to expose her to public disgrace, he had in mind to divorce her quietly. But after he had considered this, an angel of the Lord appeared to him in a dream and said, "Joseph son of David, do not be afraid to take Mary home as your wife, because what is conceived in her is from the Holy Spirit. She will give birth to a son, and you are to give him the name Jesus, because he will save his people from their sins." All this took place to fulfill what the Lord had said through the prophet:

"The virgin will conceive and give birth to a son, and they will call him Immanuel,"

which means "God with us". When Joseph woke up, he did what the angel of the Lord had commanded him and took Mary home as his wife.

✝ MATTHEW 1:19-25

✡ ISAIAH 7:14

Blessed Is the Child

At that time Mary got ready and hurried to a town in the hill country of Judea, where she entered Zechariah's home and greeted Elizabeth. When Elizabeth heard Mary's greeting, the baby leaped in her womb, and Elizabeth was filled with the Holy Spirit. In a loud voice she exclaimed: "Blessed are you among women, and blessed is the child you will bear! But why am I so favored, that the mother of my Lord should come to me? As soon as the sound of your greeting reached my ears, the baby in my womb leaped for joy. Blessed is she who has believed that the Lord would fulfill his promises to her!"

✝ LUKE 1:39-45

✡ JEREMIAH 32:22

He Has Performed Mighty Deeds

And Mary said:

"My soul glorifies the Lord
and my spirit rejoices in God my Savior,
for he has been mindful
of the humble state of his servant.
From now on all generations will call me blessed,
for the Mighty One has done great things for me—
holy is his name.
His mercy extends to those who fear him,
from generation to generation.
He has performed mighty deeds with his arm;
he has scattered those who are proud in their inmost thoughts.
He has brought down rulers from their thrones
but has lifted up the humble.
He has filled the hungry with good things
but has sent the rich away empty.
He has helped his servant Israel,
remembering to be merciful
to Abraham and his descendants forever,
just as he promised our ancestors."

Mary stayed with Elizabeth for about three months and returned home.

✝ LUKE 1:46-56

✡ 1 SAMUEL 2:1-10, PSALM 98:1

For the Lord's Hand Was with Him

When it was time for Elizabeth to have her baby, she gave birth to a son. Her neighbors and relatives heard that the Lord had shown her great mercy, and they shared her joy. On the eighth day they came to circumcise the child, and they were going to name him after his father Zechariah, but his mother spoke up and said, "No! He is to be called John."

They said to her, "There is no one among your relatives who has that name."

Then they made signs to his father, to find out what he would like to name the child. He asked for a writing tablet, and to everyone's astonishment he wrote, "His name is John." Immediately his mouth was opened and his tongue set free, and he began to speak, praising God. All the neighbors were filled with awe, and throughout the hill country of Judea people were talking about all these things. Everyone who heard this wondered about it, asking, "What then is this child going to be?" For the Lord's hand was with him.

✝ LUKE 1:57-66

✡ MALACHI 3:1, EZEKIEL 24:27

He Has Come to His People and Redeemed Them

His father Zechariah was filled with the Holy Spirit and prophesied:

"Praise be to the Lord, the God of Israel, because he has come to his people and redeemed them. He has raised up a horn of salvation for us in the house of his servant David (as he said through his holy prophets of long ago), salvation from our enemies and from the hand of all who hate us—to show mercy to our ancestors and to remember his holy covenant, the oath he swore to our father Abraham: to rescue us from the hand of our enemies, and to enable us to serve him without fear in holiness and righteousness before him all our days. And you, my child, will be called a prophet of the Most High; for you will go on before the Lord to prepare the way for him, to give his people the knowledge of salvation through the forgiveness of their sins, because of the tender mercy of our God, by which the rising sun will come to us from heaven to shine on those living in darkness and in the shadow of death, to guide our feet into the path of peace."

✝ LUKE 1:67-79

✡ 2 SAMUEL 22:3, PSALM 18:2

Born in Bethlehem

In those days Caesar Augustus issued a decree that a census should be taken of the entire Roman world. (This was the first census that took place while Quirinius was governor of Syria.) And everyone went to their own town to register. So Joseph also went up from the town of Nazareth in Galilee to Judea, to Bethlehem the town of David, because he belonged to the house and line of David. He went there to register with Mary, who was pledged to be married to him and was expecting a child. While they were there, the time came for the baby to be born, and she gave birth to her firstborn, a son. She wrapped him in cloths and placed him in a manger, because there was no guest room available for them.

✠ LUKE 2:1-7
✡ MICAH 5:2

4TH Sunday

IN ADVENT

Lord, oh how you love me. I can scarcely take in the thought that I mattered that much to you. By faith, I receive this most beautiful gift ever given to me. I look forward each day to the revelation you have for me in knowing that I am yours and that you have a plan for my life. I pray that you help me share your gift with others, especially my family and friends, for there is no greater gift I can give than sharing the gift of your love with others.

Thank you for loving me, for ransoming me and giving your life for mine.

I love you, Lord.

Good News, the Messiah Is Born

And there were shepherds living out in the fields nearby, keeping watch over their flocks at night. An angel of the Lord appeared to them, and the glory of the Lord shone around them, and they were terrified. But the angel said to them, "Do not be afraid. I bring you good news that will cause great joy for all the people. Today in the town of David a Savior has been born to you; he is the Messiah, the Lord. This will be a sign to you: You will find a baby wrapped in cloths and lying in a manger." Suddenly a great company of the heavenly host appeared with the angel, praising God and saying,

"Glory to God in the highest heaven, and on earth peace to those on whom his favor rests."

When the angels had left them and gone into heaven, the shepherds said to one another, "Let's go to Bethlehem and see this thing that has happened, which the Lord has told us about."

So they hurried off and found Mary and Joseph, and the baby, who was lying in the manger. When they had seen him, they spread the word concerning what had been told them about this child, and all who heard it were amazed at what the shepherds said to them. But Mary treasured up all these things and pondered them in her heart. The shepherds returned, glorifying and praising God for all the things they had heard and seen, which were just as they had been told.

✝ LUKE 2:8-20

✡ ISAIAH 9:6, 1 SAMUEL 16:1,
DANIEL 7:9-14

Come and Worship Him

After Jesus was born in Bethlehem in Judea, during the time of King Herod, Magi from the east came to Jerusalem and asked, "Where is the one who has been born king of the Jews? We saw his star when it rose and have come to worship him."

When King Herod heard this he was disturbed, and all Jerusalem with him. When he had called together all the people's chief priests and teachers of the law, he asked them where the Messiah was to be born. "In Bethlehem in Judea," they replied, "for this is what the prophet has written:

"'But you, Bethlehem, in the land of Judah,
   are by no means least among the rulers of Judah;
      for out of you will come a ruler
         who will shepherd my people Israel.'"

Then Herod called the Magi secretly and found out from them the exact time the star had appeared. He sent them to Bethlehem and said, "Go and search carefully for the child. As soon as you find him, report to me, so that I too may go and worship him."

After they had heard the king, they went on their way, and the star they had seen when it rose went ahead of them until it stopped over the place where the child was. When they saw the star, they were overjoyed. On coming to the house, they saw the child with his mother Mary, and they bowed down and worshiped him. Then they opened their treasures and presented him with gifts of gold, frankincense and myrrh. And having been warned in a dream not to go back to Herod, they returned to their country by another route.

✝ MATTHEW 2:1-12
✡ MICAH 5:2, NUMBERS 24:17

Christmas Day

For God so loved the world that he gave his one
and only Son, that whoever believes in him shall not
perish but have eternal life.

The thief comes only to steal and kill and destroy;
I have come that they may have life, and have it
to the full.

The Spirit of the Lord is on me, because he has
anointed me to proclaim good news to the poor.
He has sent me to proclaim freedom for the
prisoners and recovery of sight for the blind, to
set the oppressed free.

I am the way and the truth and the life.
No one comes to the Father except through me.

I am with you always, to the very end of the age.

JOHN 3:16, JOHN 10:10, LUKE 4:18,
JOHN 14:6, MATTHEW 28:20

Experience
THE REST OF
THE STORY

God goes to great lengths to rescue lost and hurting people. That is what *The Story* is all about—the story of the Bible, God's great love affair with humanity. Condensed into 31 accessible chapters, *The Story* sweeps you into the unfolding progression of Bible characters and events from Genesis to Revelation. Using the clear, accessible text of the NIV Bible, it allows the stories, poems, and teachings of the Bible to read like a novel. And like any good story, *The Story* is filled with intrigue, drama, conflict, romance and redemption—and this story's true!

**Available at TheStory.com
or wherever books are sold.**

Hardcover   9780310940974